PEOPLE WHO MADE HISTORY IN
ANCIENT GREECE

by Nicola Morgan
Illustrated by Christa Hook

RAINTREE
STECK-VAUGHN
PUBLISHERS
RSVP

A Harcourt Company

Austin   New York
www.steck-vaughn.com

Picture acknowledgments
The publisher would like to thank the following for their kind permission to use these pictures:
Ronald Sheridan, Ancient Art and Architecture Collection Ltd 21, 23, 38; A.K.G Photo, London 6, 12, 16, 21, 25, 26, 29 30, 34 (top and bottom), 37, 40, 41, 42; The Bridgeman Art Library/ Louvre, Paris/Giraudon 10/ Chartres Cathedral/Giraudon 17; C.M. Dixon 12; E.T. Archive 9, 28, 32; Hodder Wayland 5, 22, 30, 33; Michael Holford 8, 18, 24, 43; Ann Ronan at Image Select 14; Scala 36, 43; Tony Stone front cover (background); Wellcome Institute 33
Mapwork: Peter Bull

People who made history

Ancient Greece • Ancient Egypt • Ancient Rome • Native Americans

Translation from *Odyssey* (page 9) © Philip de Souza, Ph. D

Published by Raintree Steck-Vaughn Publishers, an imprint of Steck-Vaughn Company

Library of Congress Cataloging-in-Publication Data
Morgan, Nicola.
Ancient Greece / Nicola Morgan; illustrated by Christa Hook.
 p. cm.—(People who made history)
Includes bibliographical references and index.
ISBN 0-7398-2747-2
1. Greece—Civilization—To 146 B.C.—Juvenile literature.
2. Intellectuals—Greece—Biography.—Juvenile literature.
[1. Greece—Civilization—To 146 B.C.]
I. Title: People who made history in ancient greece.
II. Title. III. Series.
DF77. M7587   2000
938—dc21   00-036934

Printed in Italy. Bound in the United States.
1 2 3 4 5 6 7 8 9 0 05 04 03 02 01

Contents

Who were the ancient Greeks?

THE ANCIENT Greeks created a powerful and exciting civilization more than 2,000 years ago. Ancient Greek civilization started in about 800 B.C. and flourished until the Romans conquered it in 146 B.C., but its importance lasted for much longer.

At its height, ancient Greece covered most of the map below. Yet the importance of ancient Greece is not about how much land it covered but about what was achieved in knowledge, science, art, literature, architecture, technology, and politics.

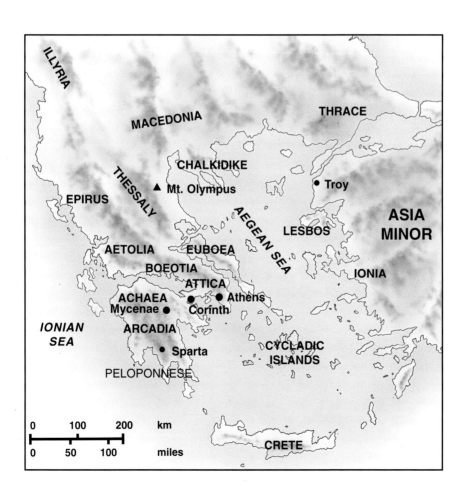

One way of understanding a civilization is to look at the individuals who made important discoveries or affected the lives of ordinary people. These men and women might have been politicians, architects, scientists, poets, or playwrights. For some of these people, we have only a few reliable details about their personal lives but it is what they achieved that is so interesting and important.

How do we know about the ancient Greeks?

We have a great deal of information about the ancient Greeks, which has been pieced together from various sources. Archaeologists have dug up buildings and found items used by the people of that time. Archaeologists have also discovered pottery and vases on which the ancient Greeks began writing from about 800 B.C. onward. Putting this all together with information from contemporary writers, including Herodotus, Thucydides, and Polybius, and also later writers, we can build up a detailed picture of what happened during this exciting time.

▲ A vase showing a man reciting poetry. Even after writing was invented, people relied on telling and listening to stories recited from memory.

ATHENS—THE KEY TO ANCIENT GREECE

At the height of its power, Athens was one of the most powerful and influential cities in the ancient world. Athens dominated Greece after the wars against Persia, (490–479 B.C.). Much of what we know about the ancient Greeks today is based on what we have discovered about this great city.

Ancient Greece in the time of Homer

WE KNOW little about Greece before 800 B.C. mainly because there is very little written down. Archaeologists have discovered the ruins of older palaces and these help us guess about earlier life in Crete and Mycenae. By 1100 B.C., these civilizations had fallen, destroyed by earthquake and war. From then until about 800 B.C., we talk about the Dark Age, because we know so little.

We believe that all the earliest poetry was oral, recited by traveling bards, who told poetic stories of gods and heroes. Nothing was written down until the Greeks developed a full alphabet around 800 B.C., borrowing the Phoenician alphabet and adding vowels.

The first poetry tells of a mythical age of heroes, when people believed that gods walked among humans. Archaeologists have found evidence of some of the places mentioned in these stories, such as Troy and Mycenae, but we can never know how much is history and how much is myth.

▲ Bronze model of a singer playing a lyre, from the eighth century B.C. Music was an important accompaniment to poetry.

STORIES ABOUT GODS AND HEROES

Gods and heroes are central to Greek myth and early history. Gods could be proud and cruel. Heroes were proud and cruel too, especially when defending their honor. Heroes didn't fear dying young, as long as they had lived with honor. If you showed disrespect for a hero he would have to punish you.

HOMER poet
circa 800 to 700 B.C.

Two of the most famous works of literature ever written are the *Iliad* and the *Odyssey*. They are said to be the work of a man named Homer. Some people believe they were written by several people; some say Homer was a woman; others deny he existed at all. We will never know for certain. However, most historians believe that Homer was a traveling poet, or bard, and that he was probably blind.

Whoever he was, or wasn't, we talk about Homer as the writer of the *Iliad* and the *Odyssey*, two epic poems that are the first known European literature. Some people even think the Greek alphabet was invented especially to record these two great poems.

▼ Homer, the bard who inspired centuries of writers with his epic poems of gods, heroes, and people —the *Iliad* and the *Odyssey*.

SPOTLIGHT ON HOMER

Name:	Homer
Nickname:	The Poet
Dates:	Nobody knows, but probably sometime between 800 and 700 B.C.
Born:	Probably Asia Minor (Turkey)
Job:	Bard
Wrote:	The *Iliad,* the *Odyssey, Battle of the Frogs* and *Mice*
Best known words:	"Rosy-fingered dawn" and "wine-dark sea"
Quote:	"Always to be the best, distinguished above the rest"
The Greeks believed:	He was blind (which may not be true)
Famous fans:	Alexander the Great used to carry his copy of Homer's work to war

The ancient Greeks certainly believed in Homer's existence and were extremely proud of him. They liked poems that described the age of heroes, and they also enjoyed Homer's powerful and beautiful language.

Homer's great poems

• The *Iliad.* Twenty-four books, each with several hundred lines, tell of a few days in the ten-year Trojan War. Whether or not this war really happened, The *Iliad* was an important tale to the ancient Greeks, especially since they won. It is an exciting story full of bloodthirsty descriptions of battles and spears piercing bodies.

• The *Odyssey.* Another twenty-four books, describing parts of Odysseus's delayed journey home after the war. His journey took nine years.

▼ This sculpture of a blind Homer was probably made in the second century A.D.

THE ODYSSEY

The opening lines of the *Odyssey* by Homer

"Sing to me, muse, of the man of many talents, who traveled far and wide after he had destroyed the holy city of Troy. Many were the men whose cities he saw, and whose thoughts he came to know. Many were the sorrows his heart endured across the seas, as he struggled to preserve his life and those of his companions."

It would take twenty-four hours to read the *Iliad* and the *Odyssey* aloud. It is difficult to imagine that these were the stories recited from a mixture of memory and invention by traveling bards.

Over 2,500 years later, we still read and study Homer's works. Besides being exciting adventures, the *Iliad* and the *Odyssey* give us another glimpse of the ancient Greek world. The tales are thrilling, funny, and sad, and sometimes they read like fairy tales, but the people and events Homer describes often seem real and true to life.

▼ The Douris Cup. A scene from the *Iliad* with the heroes Hector and Ajax fighting at Troy, each helped by a god—Apollo or Athena.

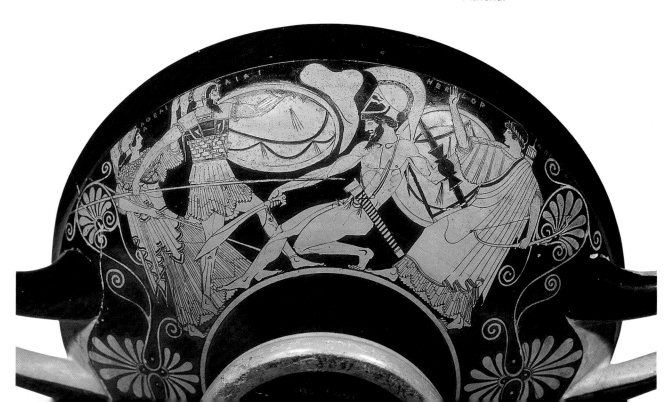

Ancient Greece in the time of Sappho

SAPPHO LIVED during the Archaic period of ancient Greece. By 594 B.C. a ruler named Solon was transforming life in Athens. When he came to power he tried to help the poor by cancelling any debts they had. He created a system of fair government. These were the first attempts in ancient Greece to build a democracy.

In addition to politics, the ancient Greeks enjoyed poetry. First there were Homer and the traveling bards who recited oral poetry. By the sixth century B.C., poetry could be written down. It developed into many different forms, styles, and rhythms. Poets themselves were highly respected and were paid for performances—many could earn a good living, much like a singer nowadays.

People believed that each area of life was the concern of a different god or goddess. The goddesses of the arts and sciences were the Nine Muses, daughters of Zeus, the king of the gods. The arts included all types of music, singing, dance, and drama. A different Muse looked after each.

▼ Relief from a Roman tomb, showing the Nine Muses. Terpsichore is the one holding a lyre.

SAPPHO

Poet
circa 620 to 580 B.C.

We remember Sappho for her beautiful poetry but we know few facts about her. She was born on the island of Lesbos and lived there most of her life. We think she probably came from a rich family because she had plenty of free time to write.

Later in life she was banished from Lesbos to Sicily because she criticized the new ruler, Pittacus, but she returned when he lost power about ten years later.

THE TENTH MUSE

"Some say there are nine Muses: but they are wrong. Look at Sappho of Lesbos; she makes ten."

Plato said this of Sappho about 200 years after she lived.

◄ Sappho, pictured with a lyre, which accompanied lyric poetry

The ancient Greeks thought Sappho was a brilliant poet. In those days it was difficult to become a famous writer or poet, especially if you were a woman. Greece was an enormous place and there were no televisions or radios, or printing presses to make copies of books. Yet Sappho was so admired in her own lifetime that coins were made showing her face. Solon, the Athenian ruler, studied one of her songs, "Because I want to learn it and die," he said.

SPOTLIGHT ON SAPPHO

Name:	Sappho
Dates:	circa 620 to 580 B.C.
Born:	Lesbos
Job:	Lyric poet
Family:	Probably married; had a daughter, named Cleis
Personality:	Emotional
Likes:	Flowers, the moon, beautiful people, strong emotions
Habit:	Poetic exaggeration—claimed that she came close to death as she looked at someone she loved

Sappho's poetry

Sappho wrote lyric poetry, which was accompanied by an instrument called a lyre. We still talk about the "lyrics" of a song. Lyric poetry describes topics like love, hate, beauty, nature, pleasure, and sadness. It expresses personal feelings and is quite different from epic poetry.

Sappho wrote nine books of poems altogether, but we only have two poems and some fragments left. Her poems are passionate, beautiful, and simple. She invented a new rhythm for verse, called a Sapphic.

◄ Stone bust of Sappho with her name below

A TASTE OF SAPPHO'S LOVE POETRY

Desire grips me yet again
I feel my legs and arms dissolve
It is overtaking me with sweet pain
All I can do is surrender

Sappho was always in love. She addressed many poems to Aphrodite, goddess of love. She was possibly the lover of Alcaeus, another famous lyric poet on Lesbos.

Many of her love poems are for girlfriends. The word lesbian originally meant "to do with love" because so much love poetry came from Lesbos. The modern meaning came later because of Sappho's love of women. The ancient Greeks were quite open about homosexuality. But later writers judged her as a dreadful woman with no morals.

There is a story about how Sappho died, which adds to the picture we have of her as a passionate and dramatic woman. It is said that she jumped to her death from a rock, because the boatman, Phaon, rejected her love. We do not know what she was really like, but we can enjoy her lovely poetry.

◄ Marble statue of Venus, the Roman goddess of love, copied from the Greek original of Aphrodite, who inspired Sappho's poetry

Ancient Greece in the time of Pythagoras

AFTER SOLON'S death in about 560 B.C., Athens was ruled by Peisistratus. Although Peisistratus was called "tyrant," he continued to improve life for many people. He encouraged art and literature and united many parts of Greece. By 508 B.C., Kleisthenes had taken control of Athens and made reforms to the constitutional structure. Meanwhile, the whole of Greece was under continued threat from the mighty Persian Empire.

Major discoveries were also being made in mathematics and astronomy. Without clocks or calendars, watching the stars and planets helps people understand time and seasons. However, to do astronomy scientifically, you need mathematics.

The Egyptians were advanced mathematicians long before the Greeks, but, as far as we know, Egyptians focused on questions like how? or what? rather than why? A Greek mathematician named Thales (circa 640 to 550 B.C.) visited Egypt and brought this practical knowledge to Greece. Thales's studies were also very useful: he predicted a solar eclipse in 585 B.C., calculated the number of days in a year, and worked out the lengths of the seasons.

► This picture from the sixteenth century A.D. shows Thales's view of a flat earth floating on water. It shows earth, water, air, and fire, from which many Greeks believed everything was made.

PYTHAGORAS
Mathematician and philosopher circa 560 to 495 B.C.

Pythagoras was absolutely passionate about his subject, mathematics. He loved the subject so much that he opened a school but could only find one pupil. He paid the pupil to stay, giving him money for each new rule he learned. The pupil was soon enjoying himself so much that when Pythagoras threatened to leave, the pupil paid Pythagoras to stay, giving him money for each new rule he taught.

Pythagoras later set up a successful school in Italy. Everyone came to his lectures, including women, although they were not normally allowed to attend places of learning. Pythagoras married one of his female followers, the beautiful and intelligent Theano. Pythagoras's pupils called themselves the Order of the Pythagoreans.

"The most noble philosopher among the Greeks."

Herodotus (485–425 B.C.), the first Greek historian, said this about Pythagoras.

▼ Pythagoras, brilliant mathematician and religious mystic

What did Pythagoras find out?

Pythagoras and his followers discovered many things about mathematics and astronomy, including:

• fractions
• odd and even numbers
• musical intervals
• square numbers, triangular numbers, and the patterns surrounding them
• that Earth is spherical
• that the planets, moon, and stars revolve in two ways

What did Pythagoras believe?

• **Religion:** Pythagoreans believed that a person's soul is immortal. If a man behaved well, his soul would return as a noble person. If he behaved badly, he would return as a pig, dog, or woman. Since any animal might contain the soul of a dead friend, Pythagoreans were vegetarian.

• **Health:** Pythagoreans followed peculiar rules for a healthy body and soul. A rule about not eating beans has an amusing possible explanation: soul was like wind, so anything that caused wind should be avoided, in case part of the soul escaped.

• **Mathematics:** Pythagoreans believed that the only way to purify the soul was through mathematics, so they studied and used it as much as they possibly could.

▶ A fifteenth century picture of Pythagoras figuring out musical notes using bells and containers of water

SPOTLIGHT ON PYTHAGORAS

Name:	Pythagoras
Dates:	circa 560 to 495 B.C.
Born:	Samos
Married:	Theano
Big mistake:	Thought the sun went around the Earth
Biggest extravagance:	So delighted when he discovered his Theorem that he sacrificed 100 oxen— hoping that they did not contain the souls of 100 friends
Famous fan:	Albert Einstein (A.D. 1879 to 1955) needed Pythagoras's Theorem for his own discoveries

RULES OF THE PYTHAGOREANS

Don't eat beans; don't walk in the main street; don't stir fire with iron; don't touch a white cockerel; don't eat a heart; don't stand on nail-clippings; don't leave an impression of your body on the bed when you get up; rub out traces of ashes in fireplace; help a man loading but not unloading; don't look in a mirror by a lamp.

▲ A stone carving of Pythagoras hard at work

Although Pythagoras is associated with some strange beliefs, he is most famous for Pythagoras's Theorem, which school children still learn today in math class. But the most important thing he did was to use mathematics to prove ideas and show why things are as they are.

SPOTLIGHT ON AESCHYLUS

Name:	Aeschylus
Nickname:	Father of Greek tragedy
Dates:	circa 525 to 456 B.C.
Born:	Eleusis near Athens
Job:	Playwright, soldier
Appearance:	Completely bald. There is a cruel (and probably untrue) story that he died when an eagle thought his shiny head was a stone and dropped a tortoise on it
Believed:	There is no heaven or hell—you will be punished or rewarded during your lifetime

Aeschylus's plays

Aeschylus wrote about ninety plays; we know the titles of eighty but only seven survive. His plays are quite different from anything that had been done before. For example, he was the first playwright to use a second actor—an idea nobody had tried before. Aeschylus also introduced costumes and scenery, making the plays more exciting.

▶ Actor's mask for use in tragedy

His most famous surviving plays are a trilogy called the *Oresteia*, which was first performed in 458 B.C. and is so powerful that it is still acted today. It tells the story of Orestes, who killed his mother, Clytemnestra, because she took a lover and killed Orestes's father, Agamemnon. Orestes is pursued and punished by the Furies, the goddesses of revenge and punishment. By the end of the third play, Orestes has been punished enough and is freed by the court of Athens and Athena, goddess of wisdom. These plays show Aeschylus's interest in justice and mercy, punishment and reward, and wisdom gained through suffering.

▼ A bronze panel showing Orestes killing his mother. Her lover is running away.

OTHER PLAYWRIGHTS

Sophocles (circa 496 to 406 B.C.) Wrote *King Oedipus, Electra, Antigone.* Interested in right and wrong. Beautiful poetry. Very popular.

Euripides (circa 485 to 406 B.C.) Wrote *Medea, The Bacchae.* Interested in psychology and why people do things. Popular after his death.

Ancient Greece in the time of Pericles

WHEN PERICLES was born, Greece was made up of many city-states all making their own rules. The Greek word for city-state was *polis*, which is where we get our word politics. Athens was the largest city-state, and sometimes the strongest, but there were other powerful city-states, such as Syracuse and Miletos.

Each city-state also had its own type of government. Most were ruled by wealthy families. A government like this was called an aristocracy. Sometimes city-states were governed by only a few men and this was called an oligarchy. Some city-states were governed by a king known as a tyrant (*tyrannos*). In all these types of government, ordinary people had little power. However, from this time, throughout Greece, city-states such as Athens were slowly introducing a form of democracy, or "rule by the people." This process was started by Solon and Kleisthenes.

City-states were often at war with each other, and with other countries, such as Persia. When Pericles was a child, Athens was in the middle of the terrible war with Persia. When Pericles was about 15, in 480 B.C., the Greeks defeated the Persians at the Battle of Salamis.

▼ This pot shows Greek citizens casting votes, watched over by the gods, including Athena, goddess of wisdom and justice.

PERICLES
Politician
circa 495 to 429 B.C.

Pericles was reelected to lead Athens nearly every year from 461 B.C. until his death in 429 BC. He kept control mainly because he was a brilliant speaker, a strong leader, and gave people what they wanted, such as paid jobs, free entertainment, and beautiful buildings.

As leader of the ruling Democratic party, Pericles changed many aspects of Athenian life. He introduced payments for members of the Assembly, so people no longer needed to be rich to play a part in politics. He spread power more widely, although women and slaves still had no power.

PERICLES'S WISDOM

On a ship when the helmsman (steering-person) was frightened by an eclipse of the sun, Pericles held his cloak over the man's eyes and asked him whether this was frightening. When the man said, "Of course not," Pericles answered, "So what is the difference between this and an eclipse, except that an eclipse is caused by something bigger than my cloak?"

Pericles used his own power over other city-states in more dishonest ways. During the war with Persia, the Delian League had been formed by Athens and other city-states so they were more of a mighty force against the Persians. After the war with the Persians ended in 449 B.C., Pericles continued to take money from his old allies for the war effort. Eventually there was lots of money saved and no war to spend it on. Pericles forced his allies to let him use much of this money to improve Athens.

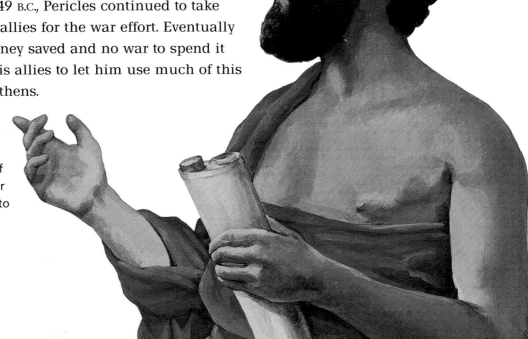

► Pericles making a speech. His brilliance at speaking saved the life of Aspasia, his mistress, after she had been sentenced to death.

SPOTLIGHT ON PERICLES

Name:	Pericles
Nickname:	The Olympian
Dates:	circa 495 to 429 B.C.
Born:	Athens
Family:	Educated, wealthy
Married:	Separated from Athenian wife; had famous mistress, Aspasia
Interests:	Making speeches, commanding warships, going to plays written by famous friends, and spending the state's money on buildings
Personality:	Never went to dinner with people to avoid seeming to favor them

Pericles's achievements

Pericles was responsible for rebuilding Athens after its war with Persia. He ordered the construction of many buildings and temples, some of which can still be seen today. The most impressive and famous is the Parthenon, a huge temple on the Acropolis, a hill in the middle of Athens. Some people, perhaps jealous of his popularity, criticized Pericles for spending so much public money on huge buildings, and also for holding expensive festivals.

◄ Aspasia, a noble woman from Miletus who was Pericles' mistress. The Athenians disliked her, partly because she had so much influence.

▲ Pericles is usually shown wearing a helmet. The story is that he had an odd-shaped skull. One writer said it was big enough to fit eleven sofas inside!

The years when Pericles was in power were called the Golden Age of Athens. This period of wealth and success began to fade in 431 B.C. when the Peloponnesian War against Sparta began. Athens eventually lost in 404 B.C. No sooner had this war started than a dreadful plague hit Athens. A year later, in 429 B.C., Pericles died of a fever.

ATHENS—THE PLACE TO BE SEEN

Pericles encouraged artists, sculptors, actors, musicians, writers, scientists, and thinkers to come to Athens. It must have been a lively place, and certainly the place to be if you wanted to see the newest play or hear the best speakers talking about exciting scientific ideas.

▼ The Parthenon, a temple to Athena, overlooking Athens. Built by Iktinos and Kallicrates on the order of Pericles

Ancient Greece in the time of Socrates

BETWEEN 431 B.C. and 404 B.C. Athens was at war with another city-state named Sparta. This was called the Peloponnesian War. In 404 B.C. the Spartans beat the Athenians. However, the Spartans allowed democracy to be reintroduced in Athens in 403 B.C.

During this time, Athens remained an important center of learning, and philosophers would come to debate in the agora. Philosophy means love of wisdom, which to the ancient Greeks meant knowledge of all sorts. Ancient Greek philosophers would discuss many things, from what the world was made of to how to behave.

The earliest philosophers focused on how the world works and what it is made of. They are called natural philosophers. They tried to explain everything without using myths: thunder is natural, they said, not the anger of Zeus. Later, philosophers focused on how to behave—once again there were many different opinions.

▼ Philosophers discussing their ideas in Aristotle's school of philosophy

SOCRATES

**Philosopher
circa 469 to 399 B.C.**

Socrates came from a wealthy Athenian family. He served in the army but spent most of his life talking and listening. Socrates is one of the most famous philosophers the world has known. He had a huge influence on later philosophers. He had a reputation for being a kindly intellectual with a good sense of humor, and he was always popular with his circle of friends.

However, people who thought they knew everything would not find Socrates so pleasant. His main opponents were the Sophists, people who claimed to be wise but often used twisted reasoning. The Sophists even charged a fee for listening to them.

SOCRATES'S OR PLATO'S IDEAS?

Socrates wrote nothing down. His famous pupil, Plato, wrote his own ideas down as conversations, but some of these ideas could have been Plato's. Even if we do not know Socrates' exact words, we know about his logical mind and his desire always to do right.

▼ Socrates searched for the answers to questions like, "What is beauty?" and "What is the best way to behave?"

SPOTLIGHT ON SOCRATES

Name:	Socrates
Nickname:	Gadfly—because he went round stinging people with his arguments and putting conceited fools in their places
Dates:	circa 469 to 399 B.C.
Born:	Athens
Job:	Philosopher
Appearance:	Homely, pot-bellied, bulging eyes, snub nose
Family:	Wealthy; mother a midwife, father a sculptor; married Xanthippe when he was 50; had three children
Personality:	Modest—in one of his famous quotes he said, "The only thing I know is that I know nothing."

His beliefs

Socrates aimed to show people that their ideas were wrong. His method was to pretend that he knew nothing and then start asking pointed questions that would lead people to say the opposite of what they had first said. We now call this "Socratic argument." Socrates often made people look foolish in public, and for this reason he made many enemies.

Apart from showing weaknesses in other people's arguments, Socrates looked for definitions of things like "happiness" and "goodness."

◄ Wall-painting of Socrates, painted in the first century A.D. It shows how unattractive he was.

▶ A painting showing Socrates about to drink the poisonous hemlock

Although Socrates said he knew nothing, he believed that it was possible to answer everything with pure reason—not through using the senses or by following the rules of society.

Socrates claimed to be guided by an inner voice that always told him what was right. This made his enemies accuse him of listening to false gods.

Socrates was eventually accused of corrupting the young with his ideas and of worshiping the wrong gods. He refused to change and was found guilty. Socrates could have chosen exile, but he preferred to die for his beliefs. He killed himself by taking hemlock, a deadly poison, to avoid giving his judges the satisfaction of executing him.

OTHER ANCIENT GREEK PHILOSOPHERS

Plato (circa 427 to 347 B.C.), Socrates's most famous pupil, and a brilliant philosopher himself. Believed that although real things change, "perfect ideas" do not. Also interested in geometry: said, "God always does geometry."

Aristotle (circa 384 to 322 B.C.), Plato's most famous pupil. Focused on the study of nature. Did not believe in Plato's "perfect ideas."

Ancient Greece in the time of Hippocrates

IN ATHENS and other parts of Greece, people were living through the turmoil of the Persian Wars, the plague in 430 B.C., and the Peloponnesian War, which Athens lost to Sparta in 404 B.C. This time also covered the Golden Age of Pericles, so it was a time of upheaval and great change.

Scientists and philosophers, such as Plato and Aristotle, were slowly discovering more about the world but there was still a great deal of superstition and ignorance.

Fortunately, the Greeks, like other ancient peoples, also realized that many plants can cure illness and that there are other practical ways of staying healthy, such as eating and exercising sensibly. Successful doctors were important and respected people and were often very highly paid.

▲ A present to the God of healing, Asclepius, to thank him for making someone's leg better. Greeks believed that the illness was cured if you pleased the gods.

◄ A doctor letting blood out of a patient. Hippocrates's ideas about "bleeding" patients lasted for hundreds of years—some doctors even do it today!

HIPPOCRATES

Doctor
circa 460 to 377 B.C.

Hippocrates's life

Very little is known about Hippocrates's life. However, we do know that Hippocrates had his own school of medicine on the island of Cos and the books we call "Hippocratic" probably came from the teachings and research from that school.

Even though we know so little about Hippocrates, he is still called the father of medicine. The reason for this is that he was the first person on record to separate medicine from religion or witchcraft. Disease was part of nature, he said, and could be treated with natural remedies, not miracles. He observed the tiniest details of symptoms and recorded these for other doctors to learn from. Hippocrates also developed rules about how doctors should behave toward patients.

▶ Hippocrates, the doctor who believed that science was the way to cure and prevent disease

THE HIPPOCRATIC OATH

Modern doctors still have to swear the Hippocratic Oath. This oath, taken from Hippocrates's teachings, describes a doctor's duty never to harm his patient and to keep secret what his patient tells him.

SPOTLIGHT ON HIPPOCRATES

Name:	Hippocrates
Nickname:	Father of Medicine
Dates:	circa 460 to 377 B.C.
Born:	Island of Cos
Job:	Doctor, teacher of other doctors
Possibly wrote:	*On Sacred Disease* (epilepsy); *Wounds in the Head; Joints; Women's Diseases*
Famous fans:	Plato and Aristotle both mention his skill and how much wealth he earned
Major achievement:	It is said that he stopped the plague in Athens by lighting fires around the city.

What Hippocrates discovered

From the Hippocratic writings, we know many interesting things he and his followers believed. They believed that four fluids, called humors, make up a body—they were blood, phlegm, yellow bile, and black bile. Illness happened when these four fluids became unbalanced. A doctor would cut his patient in a specific part of the body and let out a certain amount of blood, so that the correct humor would drain out. This theory was accepted in various countries around the world for many centuries.

► Hippocrates on a bronze coin dating from circa 50 B.C.

Of course, much of what ancient doctors thought was wrong. For example, one Hippocratic book explains that epilepsy is caused by too much phlegm and too little air in the brain, which it explains by comparing epileptics with goats, and saying that if you looked in a goat's brain you would find too much phlegm. On the other hand, much of what Hippocrates wrote about dealing with broken bones is very good medicine. The amount of detail in the books is astonishing.

WHAT HIPPOCRATES DISCOVERED...

Two things Hippocrates got right: air is carried by the veins to the limbs and the brain; extract of willow bark is a good medicine—this is the origin of aspirin, now the biggest selling medicine of all time.

Sometimes he got things wrong, claiming that people who live in fertile countries with warm climates are lazy and have bad joints.

◄ Hippocrates examining a patient in an outdoor clinic. The doctor always seems to be sitting down.

▼ Ancient surgical instruments from Greek and Roman times

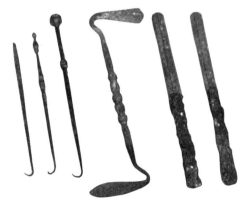

Ancient Greece in the time of Alexander the Great

WAR WITH each other as well as war against Persia left the city-states of Athens and Sparta considerably weakened. By the fourth century B.C. Athens was beginning to flourish again but it was no longer powerful enough to unite the Greek city-states and create a Greek empire.

Macedonia was a country to the north of Greece, which the Greeks had largely ignored. However, from 359 B.C. on, Philip II of Macedon had been building up his country to make it more powerful. He wanted to destroy the mighty Persian Empire and to do this he needed control of Greece. In 338 B.C. Philip and his army beat the Greek army at the battle of Chaeronea and took over Greece. Less than a year later he was ready to fight against Persia. In Athens, many people did not like being ruled by Macedonians, whom they called "barbarians," but they had little choice.

Philip II was Alexander's father and Alexander inherited Philip's desire to conquer the Persians and to rule as much of the world as possible.

▼ Gold medallion showing Philip II of Macedon (circa 382 to 336 B.C.), father of Alexander the Great

▼ Detail from a tomb called the Alexander Sarcophagus. It shows a Greek rider, believed to be Alexander, from about 330 B.C.

ALEXANDER

General
circa 356 to 323 B.C.

Alexander expected to excel at everything. At age 14, he tamed a wild stallion, Bucephalus, after his father said the horse was too wild to ride. His chief private tutor, Leonidas, set harsh standards: he believed that the healthiest breakfast was a walk before dawn, and would check Alexander's bag in case his mother had slipped a snack into it. Alexander was also taught briefly by Aristotle, though they argued later on—perhaps when Alexander executed Aristotle's nephew Kallisthenes for disagreeing with him.

Alexander was sixteen when he was first left in charge of Macedonia and eighteen when he fought his first battle. Immediately afterward, he visited Athens for the only time in his life, which is remarkable considering that he became ruler of Greece.

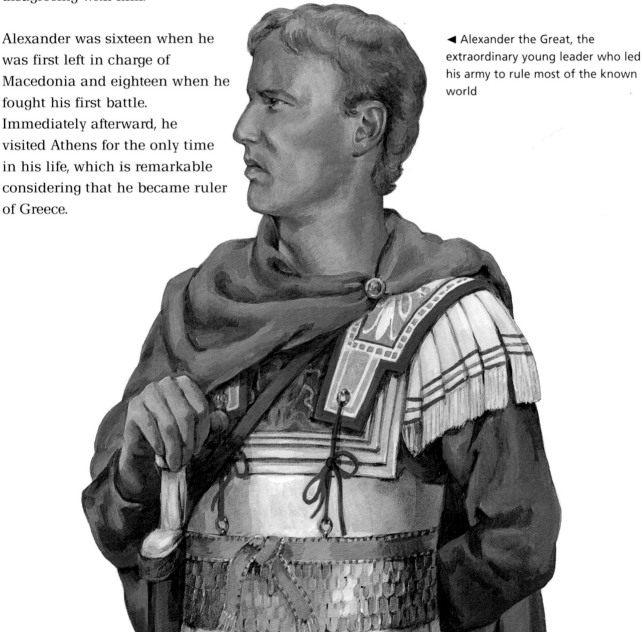

◄ Alexander the Great, the extraordinary young leader who led his army to rule most of the known world

SPOTLIGHT ON ALEXANDER THE GREAT

Name:	Alexander
Nickname:	The Great
Dates:	circa 356 to 323 B.C.
Born:	Macedon
Parents:	Philip II and Olympias
Job:	King, general
Features:	Muscles, lots of scars
Best friend:	Hephaestion
Horse:	Bucephalus
Wives:	Roxana, Stateira, and Parysatis (Polygamy, or marrying more than one woman at a time, was a Macedonian royal custom)

Alexander became king at the age of nineteen after his father's assassination. He was thirty-three when he died of a fever, but in those fourteen years he conquered much of the known world, including Persia, Asia Minor, Egypt, and India up to the Ganges River. Here he had to stop because his men refused to go farther. He sulked in his tent for days, but eventually agreed to go back.

► This Renaissance painting is an interpretation of the marriage of Alexander to Roxana. Alexander admired her great beauty.

◄ This mosaic, called *"The Alexander Battle,"* shows Alexander fighting the Persian king, Darius III, at the Battle of Issos.

Modern historians disagree about whether Alexander just wanted to conquer the world or whether he wanted East and West to live in peace and learn from each other. He was intelligent, brave, and a brilliant leader, and his soldiers adored him. However, he had a dark side. He killed his own foster brother, Kleitus, in a drunken fight, and burned down a palace during a party. Sometimes he was accused of not being truly Greek, because he adopted Eastern habits.

Whatever his faults, he succeeded in his mission: to destroy the Persian empire and replace it with a strengthened Greek one.

ALEXANDER'S LOVE OF KNOWLEDGE

Alexander did not always destroy the places he conquered. He loved knowledge, so in many places he created libraries and centers of learning. For example, he created the city of Alexandria, in Egypt, which became a world center of knowledge for hundreds of years. He also carried a copy of Homer's *Iliad* into every battle.

Ancient Greece in the time of Archimedes

U NDER ALEXANDER the Great, the Greek Empire had spread to new areas, including Asia Minor, Afghanistan, Iraq, Iran, India, and Egypt. In all of these lands new cities were formed and the people there adopted many Greek ways, including democracy.

The Greeks also influenced the way people questioned the world around them and then found answers to those questions. The word "science" comes from the Latin word for "knowledge;" scientists look for what can be known about the world. They can use what earlier scientists discover, but the earliest Greeks had to start from almost nothing.

At first, philosophy, mathematics, astronomy, the study of nature and all the sciences were mixed together. Early scientists were often wrong but, when you consider how they started from nothing and how little they had in the way of instruments, this is unsurprising. Some of their ideas seem foolish today but our knowledge comes from hundreds of years of work, and the Greeks were a huge part of that work.

► This Roman relief shows a crane, similar to those in Archimedes's early designs, being used to build the Aterii monument in Rome in the first century B.C.

ARCHIMEDES

Scientist
circa 287 to 212 B.C.

Archimedes came from an educated family. He was the son of an astronomer, Pheidias, and was related to the king of Syracuse, Hieron II. He was born and lived in Syracuse, though he also studied in Alexandria.

Many of Archimedes's findings have turned out to be right. The sixteenth century scientist, Copernicus, and Galileo in the seventeenth century both used his discoveries. He had the ability to see things in his mind and then to prove them mathematically. This new method of starting with a theory and then setting out to prove or disprove it is why he is sometimes called "the first scientist."

A few of Archimedes's discoveries:
- understood the principle of levers and pulleys (like those in a crane) to move huge objects
- calculated areas and volumes
- predicted eclipses, measured distances to stars, made a planetarium, measured the year
- created machines such as the Archimedean Screw, which could raise water from a lower level to a higher level

ARCHIMEDES'S INVENTIVE MACHINES

Archimedes was enormously respected, even by his enemies. He designed cranes with mechanical claws, which lifted enemy ships out of the water and catapults that could hurl rocks of more than a ton. The Romans would often flee if they saw one of his machines about to be used against them.

◄ Archimedes, sometimes called "the first scientist." He had the ability to visualize scientific principles and make them work.

SPOTLIGHT ON ARCHIMEDES

Name:	Archimedes
Dates:	circa 287 to 212 B.C.
Born:	Syracuse (Sicily)
Job:	Scientist
Personality:	Excitable, super-intelligent
Famous future fans:	Galileo, Copernicus, Isaac Newton
Quote:	"Give me a firm spot on which to stand and I will move the Earth" (referring to the principle of the lever)
Impressive trick:	Moved a ship over dry land, using one hand and a pulley

▲ A sixteenth century engraving showing Archimedes in his bath. You can see the crown and weights, as well as a container to collect the water that overflowed.

"Eureka"

The most famous story about Archimedes is the *"eureka"* one. Though it is probably not entirely true, it gives us a clue to Archimedes's personality and one of his most important discoveries. King Hieron had asked Archimedes to discover whether his jeweler had cheated by making his crown with less gold and more silver. Archimedes puzzled over this in the bath. Observing that his body made the water rise, he realized something amazing. He leaped out and ran naked through the streets excitedly shouting *"eureka!"* Greek for "I've found it!"

Archimedes had realized that he could weigh the crown, then find a piece of gold that weighed the same. He could then find out whether the crown was made completely of gold by seeing if each made the same amount of water overflow when placed in a bowl full of water. We believe that the jeweler was guilty but Archimedes would have been much more interested in the scientific principle he had discovered.

Archimedes died as he had lived: obsessed with his work. When the Romans took control of his home town, Syracuse, he continued to work. When a Roman soldier met him, Archimedes refused to move until he had finished a calculation. The soldier, who didn't recognize him, drew his sword and killed him.

▲ A mosaic showing a Roman soldier about to kill Archimedes while he works

How did it all end?

DURING THE two hundred years after Alexander the Great, the Romans were growing in strength. They began conquering Greek city-states in Southern Italy. In 168 B.C. they conquered Macedonia, but in 146 B.C. the Romans conquered the rich Greek city-state of Corinth. Greece was no longer the powerful country it had been.

However, the Romans did not destroy the great culture they found—they took it for themselves and before long the Romans were learning Greek too. Romans admired and copied Greek architecture, literature, theater, philosophy, and science, and many aspects of the Greek way of life. When the Romans went on to further conquests, they took Greek achievements with them wherever they went. So, even though Greeks ceased ruling themselves, their civilization and achievements continue to be important right up to the present day.

▼ A Roman mosaic from the third century A.D., showing a scene from Homer's *Odyssey*: Odysseus being tempted by the Sirens

It is amazing to think how much the ancient Greeks continue to influence our lives: democracy is the system of government in many countries; modern physics and mathematics still use rules discovered by Greeks such as Thales, Pythagoras, and Archimedes; much modern architecture in the cities of Europe and the United States is copied from their buildings; western philosophy is hugely influenced by the works of Socrates, Plato, and Aristotle; modern literature is full of references to ancient Greek writers. Western languages, including English, are dotted with ancient Greek words, and in schools and universities all over the world people still read ancient Greek literature and even learn the language of classical Greece.

"I say someone in another time will remember us."
Sappho

▲ When Athenians wanted to get rid of a politician they wrote his name on a piece of broken pottery called an "ostrakon." The person with the most "votes" was banished. Today, we use the word "ostracize" to mean to ignore or shun.

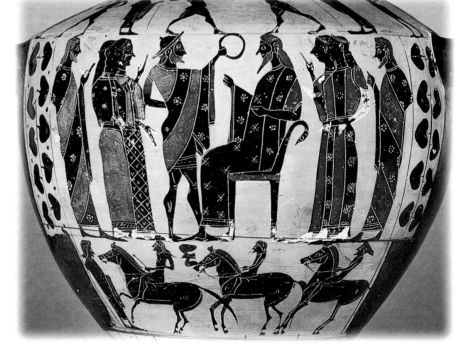

► A vase from the fifth century B.C. shows a victorious athlete being crowned with a wreath, just as athletes today are awarded prizes or medals at competitions, such as the Olympics.

Time Line

Bronze Age (3000 to 1100 B.C.)

3000–1100	Minoan civilization on Crete
	(some palaces destroyed in 1700, possibly by earthquake)
2000	First Greek-speaking people arrive on mainland Greece
1600	Rise of Mycenaean culture on mainland
1200	Possible date of Trojan War. Some Mycenaean palaces fall

Dark Age (1100 to 800 B.C.)

by 1100	Mycenaean and Minoan cultures have fallen
900–800	Greeks travel more widely and build Greek city-states in Asia Minor

Archaic Period (800 to 500 B.C.)

800	Greeks adapt Phoenician alphabet, introducing vowels
800–700	Probable dates of Homer
776	First Olympic games
750	Greeks continue to expand into Italy and Black Sea area
638–559	Solon
620–580	Probable dates of Sappho
585	Thales (640 to 550 B.C.) predicts eclipse
	of sun
584–495	Probable dates of Pythagoras
545	Persians expand into Greece;
	Peisistratus tyrant in Athens until 527 B.C.
525–456	Probable dates of Aeschylus
508	Democracy introduced in Athens by
	Kleisthenes

Classical Age (500 to 323 B.C.)

500–449	Persian Wars; Greeks win at Marathon (490 B.C.) and Salamis (480 B.C.)
495–429	Probable dates of Pericles
478–432	Athens's greatest period
469–399	Probable dates of Socrates
460–377	Probable dates of Hippocrates
431–404	Peloponnesian War between Athens and Sparta (Sparta wins)
430	Plague in Athens
359	Philip II becomes king of Macedon
338	Philip II rules Greece as head of League of Corinth
356–323	Probable dates of Alexander the Great
322	Athenian democracy ends

Hellenistic Period (322 to 331 B.C.)

287–212	Probable dates of Archimedes
212	Rome defeats Syracuse and takes over Sicily
211–205	Macedonians at war with Rome (also 202 to 197 and 171 to 168)
168	Rome defeats Macedonia
146	Rome defeats Corinth—Greece now ruled by Rome
31	Rome wins battle of Actium—last Hellenistic ruler defeated. Rome now rules Egypt, Macedonia, Greece, and much of Europe, Africa, and Asia

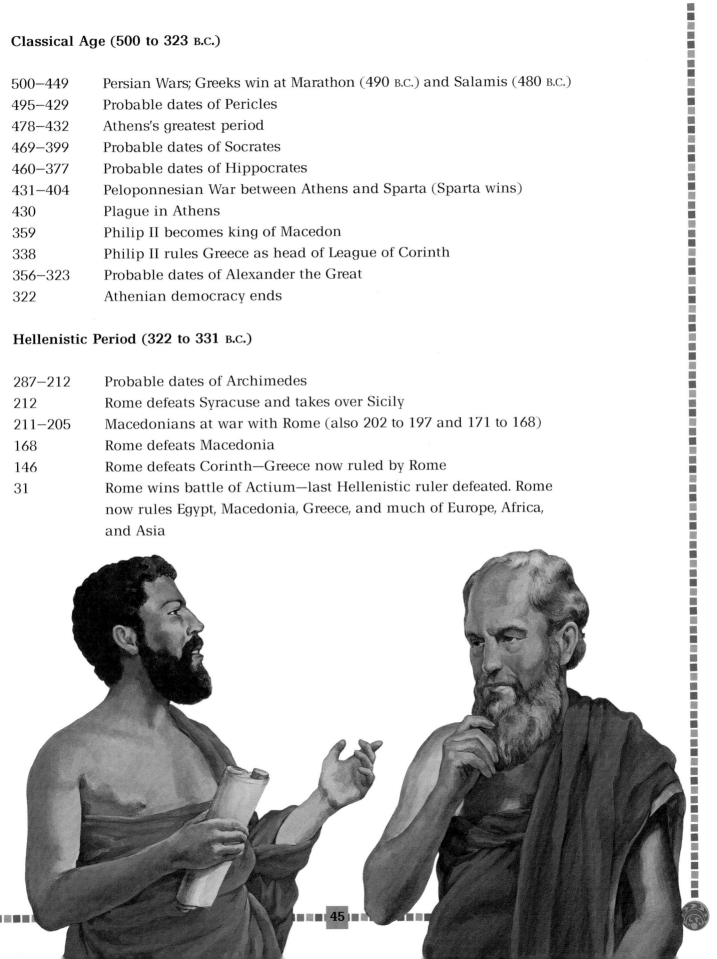

Glossary

agora The marketplace, where public meetings were often held.

archaeologist Person whose job is to dig up things from the past.

architecture Style of buildings.

aristocracy Powerful class of wealthy or important families, from the words *aristos* (best) and *kratos* (power).

aristocrat A member of one of the ruling families.

banished Sent to another country as a punishment.

barbarians Originally anyone from the North, or anyone whom the Athenians considered uncivilized because their language sounded like "bar bar."

bard A poet who tells stories using poetry and music.

circa Around, about, approximately. Used with dates.

democracy Government by the people. In Greek terms this meant allowing the citizens to make their own decisions rather than their leaders.

epic Long story-poem, about heroes, gods, and ancient stories.

Furies Three frightening half-goddesses whose job was to punish murderers, especially those who murdered a relative; also called the "Eumenides" or "kindly ones."

geometry The mathematics of shapes and angles.

immortal Living forever; undying.

literature Written work that represents a particular civilization, including its poetry, history, and drama.

lyre Musical instrument like a small harp.

lyric Type of poetry that is accompanied by a lyre.

myth A traditional, not factual, story about historical events.

mythical From a myth.

oligarchy Rule by a few people chosen by each other.

oral Spoken, not written down.

ostracize To banish a politician after the people have voted to reject him.

philosophy Love of wisdom—and Greek wisdom included every type of knowledge and inquiry.

playwright Someone who writes plays.

tragedy Type of drama; typically about the fall of a great man.

trilogy Three plays making a complete story.

Further information

Pronunciation guide

Emphasize the syllable in bold

Aeschylus	**Ess**-kuh-lus
Aphrodite	A-froh-**die**-tee
Archimedes	Ar-kuh-**me**-dees
Aristotle	**Ar**-uh-sto-tul
Athena	A-**thee**-nuh
Einstein	**Ine**-stine
Euripides	Yu-**ri**-puh-deez
Galileo	Ga-luh-**lay**-oh
Heracles	**Hair**-uh-kleez
Herodotus	Heh-**rod**-ot-us
Hieron	Hee-**air**-on
Hippocrates	Hip-**pa**-kra-teez
Kleisthenes	**Klys**-then-eez
Iliad	**Ill**-ee-ad
Mycenae	My-**see**-nee
Odysseus	O-**dis**-ee-us
Odyssey	**Ah**-di-see
Orestes	Uh-**res**-tees
Peloponnesian	Pel-op-on-**ee**-zhun
Pericles	**Per**-i-kleez
Pheidias	**Fy**-dee-as
Plato	**Play**-toh
Pythagoras	Puh-**tha**-guh-rus
Roxana	Rox-**ah**-na
Sappho	**Sa**-fo
Socrates	**Sah**-kruh-tees
Solon	**Soh**-lon
Sophocles	**Sah**-fuh-klees
Syracuse	**Sir**-a-kuse
Thales	**Thay**-leez
Zeus	**Zooss**

Books to read

Chrisp, Peter. *Look Inside a Greek Theater.* Raintree Steck-Vaughn, 2000.

Crosher, Judith. *Technology in the Time of Ancient Greece.* Raintree Steck-Vaughn, 1998.

Dawson, Imogen. *Food and Feasts in Ancient Greece* (Food and Feasts). Silver Burdett Press, 1993.

Hull, Robert. *Greece* (The Ancient World). Raintree Steck-Vaughn, 1998.

Loverance, Rowena. *Ancient Greece* (See Through History). Viking Children's Books, 1993.

Millard A. & S. Peach. *The Greeks* (Illustrated World History). Millbrook Press, 1990.

Pearson, Anne. *Everyday Life in Ancient Greece* (Clues to the Past). Franklin Watts, 1994.

Websites

These sites provide excellent sources of information about all aspects of ancient Greek history, literature, and people:

http://www.museum.upenn.edu
http://argos.evansville.edu
http://www.perseus.tufts.edu

Index